busi ness blurb.
365 DAYS OF BUSINESS IDEAS

FOR TEEN ENTREPRENEURS

DEDICATION:

To you, the young entrepreneur.

ACKNOWLEDGEMENTS:

The Business Blurb Editorial Team wrote this book in the hopes of having a positive influence on young, aspiring entrepreneurs. As a company, our sole goal is to educate, inspire and entertain entrepreneurs globally and we hope this book does just that. Ultimately, if we can play a role in sparking that million-dollar idea then we achieved our goal

IDEA NO. 1

Social Media Influencer

If you are skilled in social media, build a solid personal brand surrounding a specific niche. Once you gain a strong enough audience, you can monetize your following.

Being a social media influencer can be lucrative. You can earn from brand deals, selling merchandise, affiliate links, and so much more. You can make money by creating and posting sponsored content for brands you collaborate with.

IDEA NO. 2

Tutor

Whether you're good at math, English, science, or reading, leverage your skills to teach someone else who may be struggling in that class.

Tutoring is an easy way to make some extra cash. You can earn some solid cash from tutoring online students using any platform. If you get overly busy, consider outsourcing some jobs to your friends and taking a service fee.

IDEA NO. 3

Mobile Car Detailing

Are you interested in cars? Purchase some supplies and educate yourself on the different chemicals to make a used car look new. It is a lucrative business opportunity as every car, pick-up truck, van, minivan, and even motorcycle is a potential customer.

Advertise your service in local Facebook groups with impressive before and after photos. Before you know it, you will be booked.

IDEA NO. 4

Dog Walking

Love dogs? A dog walking business is an easy way to make some extra cash by walking some furry friends.

Dog walking offers flexible hours and is essentially all profit as your clients will provide everything necessary. It is a great side gig since there is no exclusive training or certification required.

IDEA NO. 5

Mulching

If you live in a populated town, go door to door and see if any of your neighbors are interested in having you mulch around their house. You can mulch gardens, trees, shrubs, and even their lawns.

Make sure to take before and after photos to show the difference between unmulched and mulched beds to intrigue other customers.

IDEA NO. 6

Cutting Lawns

Mowing lawns is a great business and is constantly in demand as everyone needs lawn care. You can expand your business by offering to mow the lawn and then build on top of that with landscaping, sod installation, gardening, weeding, or tree trimming.

Use Facebook to reach out to residents in your area to ask them if you can cut their lawn. Use social media to showcase your work to close the next deal.

IDEA NO. 7

Weeding Houses

Love landscaping? Consider bringing in some extra dough by weeding your neighbor's flower beds.

Use social media to showcase your work and find new customers in your area.

IDEA NO. 8

Interior House Painting

Painting the interior of houses is a great way to earn money. Not only is there always a solid market for house painting, but word of mouth will spread quickly when you do a job well.

Offer to paint a friend, family member, or neighbors' room as a test and take photos before, during, and after you paint. Post these photos in a local Facebook group or advertise to intrigue new customers.

IDEA NO. 9

Moving Furniture

Are you and your friends strong and looking to get paid to get a workout in? People are constantly in need of strong teenagers to move their furniture.

Consider gathering some friends together and starting a furniture moving business. Spread the word locally through social media and handing out flyers.

IDEA NO. 10

House Cleaning

Do you help out with your chores at home and want to apply those skills elsewhere? Start a house cleaning business and charge a weekly retainer to your customers. Do a cost analysis beforehand to figure out what you will have to pay for business cards, flyers, materials, licenses, gasoline, equipment, and other overhead items.

Leveraging dramatic before and after photos is an excellent way to attract new clients to your house cleaning business.

IDEA NO. 11
Babysitter

Love working with kids? Child care is constantly in need and can be a lucrative industry. It is a flexible and well-paid part-time job.

Let local families know your availability and set up a calendar where you can book and track your jobs. If you become overly busy, consider starting a babysitting company that connects locals to babysitters in the area.

IDEA NO. 12

Running Errands

Adults are constantly busy juggling a hefty work schedule or taking their kids to activities. Start an errand-running business to take some stress off local parents.

Whether this means grabbing groceries, delivering dinner, or something else, make it your priority to lighten their load. It is possible to earn tens of thousands of dollars in a year running errands for money.

IDEA NO. 13

Music Lessons

Talented musically? If you're passionate about playing music, connect with local music teachers to see if they have any students that would be interested in lessons.

It is a viable business IDEA NO. for musically inclined teens and will be easy to get repeat customers. You could choose to do it full time or combine online lessons with face-to-face ones.

IDEA NO. 14

Youtuber

Did you grow up dreaming of being an influencer? Stop dreaming and start doing! Build a YouTube channel around your life, personality, or passion. You can earn money on YouTube by applying for and being accepted to the YouTube Partner Program.

Don't get down on yourself if the views don't come in immediately. YouTube is a highly competitive platform, and it can take years of hard work and dedication to grow a channel.

IDEA NO. 15

Elder Tech Help

Are you constantly on your phone? Create a business that helps older folks set up smartphones and connect with their families on social media.

Although using your phone is a piece of cake for you, it's not the same for older people. Many elders could use your help with their smart devices to stay connected to loved ones, engage via virtual experiences, and even age in place.

IDEA NO. 16

Graphic Designer

Do you have an eye for logos, colors, and overall branding? Graphic design may just be for you. You can create and sell templates online and even market your products.

Starting a graphic design business is as easy as teaching yourself some basic skills and cold-emailing some businesses that may use your help!

IDEA NO. 17

Candle Business

Are you addicted to buying candles? Start a candle business. Candles are constantly in demand, and there are endless scents when it comes to the candle business. You can make candles at home as a hobby and turn them into a profitable business.

A candle business can be a fun way to get your creative juices flowing through unique designs, scents, and so much more.

IDEA NO. 18

Freelance Writer

Are you an A+ English student who enjoys writing? Freelancing writing is constantly in demand as more and more publications seek to cover various topics on the internet. You can get paid to write articles for blogs, magazines, and journals.

Whether you start a freelance writing company or freelance yourself, make sure to build out a portfolio and stick to covering niches that you genuinely take an interest in.

IDEA NO. 19

Website Expert

Web expert? Creating websites for smaller businesses in your area can be a fun and rewarding money maker. You need to define your goal and the target market to attract suitable investors.

Being a website expert is a great way to express your talents to the public and assist small companies.

IDEA NO. 20

Photographer

Love taking pictures? Being a photographer is a great way to rack up some cash. You can take a walk around your neighborhood and speak to business owners about what you do and how you can help them attract more clients with stunning photos.

Use Instagram to create a portfolio and showcase your work to your friends, family, and potential customers.

IDEA NO. 21

Transcription

Are you a skilled typist and love working from the comfort of your own home? Transcription might just be for you. Transcription jobs could range from creating a transcription of recorded interviews and focus groups to lectures and podcasts. You can work as much as you want, from wherever you want.

With subtitles becoming a more and more popular tool, transcription is in demand. Tons of online sites will pay you to transcribe video and audio clips.

IDEA NO. 22

Create an App

If you're into coding, building an app is a perfect way to express your creativity. Mobile applications are an excellent way for business owners to improve their company and outsource you for the purpose.

Whether creating a fun game or building a platform that can solve a problem, creating an app could be the right direction in the future.

IDEA NO. 23

Live Streamer

If you like technology and you think you're entertaining, live streaming could be a perfect route to go.

Once you have an audience on one of the various streaming platforms, you can start monetizing your audience through merchandise, donations, subscribers, and brand integrations.

IDEA NO. 24

Homemade Goods

If you're a fan of arts and crafts, making homemade goods and reselling them on Etsy is a great business to start at any age. You can make your own jewellery, homemade cards, print t-shirts, upcycle things around the house, or even make beautiful terrariums to sell on sites.

Leverage social media by showing your process, packing products that you have made by hand.

IDEA NO. 25

Craft Vendor

Do you enjoy crafts? Consider selling Craft kits with everything you need in one bundle.

It will make crafts easier for busy parents who don't have time to shop for various crafting necessities. With Facebook groups, buy/trade/sell groups, using a blog or Etsy, you can open up a shop and start making crafts to sell!

IDEA NO. 26

Print On Demand

Create a print-on-demand store surrounding a specific niche and run targeted advertisements to promote your shop.

Print on demand is a more affordable way to create an online store as you do not need to invest in any kind of inventory.

IDEA NO. 27

Gift Baskets

Curating custom gift baskets or party favors for special events is an excellent way to compile different items into a visually appealing gift!

Targeting moms through Facebook is your best bet for this business. Include branded cards with your company's name in each basket as free advertising to meet the taste of the individual who receives them.

IDEA NO. 28

Kid's Taxi

Create a Kid's Taxi service where multiple parents chip in to have their kids dropped off and picked up from school, sporting events, and extracurricular activities.

Although this business carries a heavy responsibility, it can be highly lucrative as multiple parents are chipped in for the rideshare.

IDEA NO. 29

Social Media Consultant

If social media is your thing, consider starting a social media consultant business. It is where you can guide smaller businesses on growing and building a robust digital footprint by leveraging social media.

Start by looking for businesses that lack a strong social media presence and reach out to them. Explain the value of your service and showcase your previous work to your customers.

IDEA NO. 30

Sneaker Reseller

If you're a fan of sneakers, start reselling your favorite shoes online or at sneaker conventions.

Use Twitter and other online resources to find out the latest rare sneaker releases. Make sure you're the first ones on the site or wait in line at participating stores. Once you secure them, flip your shoes for a hefty profit!

IDEA NO. 31

Garage Sale Organizer

Everyone likes getting rid of old stuff, but no one has the time to organize a garage sale. A garage sale organizer is an excellent side hustle to help others liquidate their junk. With simple garage organization steps, along with some clever storage solutions, you can get the most out of this gig.

You can offer pricing items, promote the sale, and attract locals through Facebook groups. Charge an hourly fee or a percentage of the sales you can acquire.

IDEA NO. 32

Disc Jockey

Love music? Invest in some DJ equipment and offer your services for block parties, birthdays, bat mitzvahs, and other special occasions.

Whether you charge an hourly rate or a fixed cost, becoming a disc jockey can be very profitable.

IDEA NO. 33

Garbage Bin Cleaner

Believe it or not, starting a garbage bin cleaning company can be highly profitable. Whether you invest in a truck or simply use a power washer, create a subscription where clients get their trash cans cleaned once a month.

Leverage social media and use before and after photos to show the actual value of your services.

IDEA NO. 34

Streetwear Brand

Are you a so-called hypebeast? Consider starting a streetwear brand of your own. Starting a streetwear brand can be gratifying work. After all, you are solving an immediate issue for your customer, and you're working on something you genuinely care about.

Don't forget there are millions of clothing companies, so ensure yours is unique in its own way.

IDEA NO. 35

Vending Machine Operator

Interested in something that will make you passive income and have some money saved up? Purchase a vending machine and reach out to local businesses to see if they will let you put it on their property.

Although your upfront fee is a bit pricey, vending machines can be an excellent long-term investment and take much less work than some other side hustles.

IDEA NO. 36

Virtual Assistant

Love working from home? Consider starting a VA business. Virtual assistants are typically independent contractors that provide an array of administrative services.

If you aren't interested in becoming a VA yourself, start a VA sourcing business to connect business owners with VA's and take a service fee.

IDEA NO. 37
Video Editor

Are you a talented video editor? Put these skills to use by starting a video editing company. You don't even need a studio to become a successful video editor. Powerful laptops can now handle many of the tasks that editors used to perform in a studio.

With videos becoming a more and more prominent way to digest information, video editing is definitely in need.

IDEA NO. 38
Fitness Trainer

Are you a gym rat? Get paid to work out and teach others your fitness techniques. Working as a trainer, you have two main choices, leading to a good salary: work for someone else or start your own training business to see clients. You can make good money either way.

Whether you offer group sessions or one-on-one coaching, teaching others how to get fit can be extremely satisfying once you see results.

IDEA NO. 39

Moving Assistant

Moving is stressful for everyone. You can ease people's lives and start a moving assistant business to help others organize and execute their moves.

It is preferable for smaller moves where the client rents a truck and you and your friends can load and unload furniture. You can increase your income by offering other services, including wrapping, padding, and securing belongings in a moving truck.

IDEA NO. 40

Facebook Marketplace Seller

People constantly have items they are looking to sell but don't have the patience for Facebook Marketplace. Start a business where you list and execute the sales of their items and take a service fee.

This is a highly high-paying service, top-rated in highly populated towns.

IDEA NO. 41

Blogger

Love writing? Choose a niche and start your own blog surrounding something you are passionate about. You can use WordPress and blogging to earn money online by doing what you love. You can work from home, on your own time, and there is no limit on how much money you can make.

Monetize your website with advertisements, affiliate links, and brand partnerships.

IDEA NO. 42

Inventor

Are you creative and constantly thinking of brilliant inventions? Create something new that solves a problem.

The best way to go about this is to list five problems you run into daily and create IDEA NO.s with practical solutions to these issues.

IDEA NO. 43

House-Sitting Business

Are your neighbors going away for vacation and looking for someone to keep an eye on their house? Start a house-sitting business.

This may entail bringing in mail, packages and possibly even watering their flowers or maintaining the lawn.

IDEA NO. 44

Computer Set-up Service

Computers can be complicated to set up. If you have knowledge and experience in keeping computers up and running, you can start a computer set-up business quickly and affordably. Help others transfer their old files, applications, and documents to their new computer.

Make sure to explain how everything works and ensure they don't have any questions before you leave.

IDEA NO. 45

Portrait Artist

Is art your thing? Becoming a freelance artist can be an excellent gig to keep you busy. Leverage social media to show off your portfolio and list your services on Etsy to drive more sales.

And if you are the proactive and extrovert type of artist, finding students shouldn't be a problem. But first, you have to establish which type of teaching will be more suitable for you.

IDEA NO. 46

Sublimation

Love designing and want to earn some extra money? Whether you're looking to start your first business or if you already own a decorating business, sublimation is a great business to get into.

By creating fabulous and personalized items for family members, local groups on Facebook, or even Etsy, marketing on social media is the way to go.

IDEA NO. 47

Parking Service

Have too much time on your hands? Having a parking service business is a great way to earn passive income.

This business can be a bit pricey to start but highly useful in populated areas.

IDEA NO. 48

Proofreader

Love reading? Do you have an eye for spotting typos and an irresistible urge to fix them? If so, becoming a proofreader is an excellent gig to keep yourself busy.

Leveraging social media such as LinkedIn and having a website to show off your skills is a great way to find new clients.

IDEA NO. 49

Leaf Raking Business

Who says money doesn't grow on trees? If your parents ever paid you to rake the leaves, you know there's green in those red and orange beauties. When the fall colors start to turn, it's time to think about making a little extra cash by getting into the leaf-raking business. You can start a leaf removal business to help out the people in your area.

Taking pictures before and after your work on social media is a great way to find new customers in your area.

IDEA NO. 50

Personal Shopper

Love fashion? Becoming a personal shopper is an excellent way to boost someone's confidence and earn some money.

Using social media to have pictures of your clients to showcase and represent your fashion knowledge is a great way to expand your brand.

IDEA NO. 51

Junk Removal

People constantly have junk at their house that they don't know what to do with. Start a business in your area that provides a service to remove junk. You can start with the basics, figure out the travel time to and from the pickup location, and then the eventual disposal site.

Market your service on Facebook and join your town's group chats to find new clients and showcase your business.

IDEA NO. 52

Clean Garages

Love cleaning? Start a garage business in your free time and earn some extra cash. You can clean, restock, organize, inspect, and repair the garage. You can also offer other services while cleaning the garage, such as cleaning their house or tending to their lawn for an extra fee.

Leverage social media to your advantage and start contacting people on Facebook to see if they are interested in your service.

IDEA NO. 53

Face Paint

Do you enjoy painting faces as a hobby? Can you work with children and adults? If so, you might be able to turn your artistic hobby into a money-making opportunity. At first, it may be difficult to generate a regular income. But if you are open to all jobs, big or small, you will soon build up a network of people who will recommend you and your face painting skills.

Having pictures on social media of your work is a great way to leverage your service to potential customers in your area.

IDEA NO. 54

Movie Screen Rental

Love movies? Start a movie screen rental business in your area. You can start this gig by purchasing a few backyard theater systems and then charge a daily rental fee for individuals and organizations who need such a system for an isolated event.

Offer your service on Facebook and run ads through people in your area that might be the potential customers.

IDEA NO. 55

Pool Cleaner

Are you bored in the summer and want to earn extra cash? Starting a pool cleaning business is a simple and easy way to do it.

Leverage social media to take before and after pictures of your work and express yourself on social media so you can target potential customers that have a pool.

IDEA NO. 56

Furniture Restoration

Everyone's always looking to upgrade their furniture. Starting a furniture repair business in your area is an excellent way to earn some money and save the environment.

By using the Facebook marketplace, you can advertise your new furniture and find potential customers. Etsy and craigslist is also a good place to sell your items to earn some money.

IDEA NO. 57

PR Firm

Are you good at communication? Starting a PR firm is right in your alley where you can show off your creativity and earn some good income. If starting up your firm is too big a step, then being freelance can be lucrative too.

Leveraging social media connections to media outlets is a great way to pick up new clients and provide them with a service such as press that will help out both parties.

IDEA NO. 58

Marketing Agency

Love building brands on social media? Building a marketing agency is the perfect business for you.

Reach out to occupations in your area looking to expand their social media presence, such as dentists, lawyers, etc. Remember, you have to provide proof on social media so your clients can trust you.

Homework Helper

Love school? Becoming a homework helper is a great way to earn some extra cash and help out students in your school.

Use your knowledge to help out younger students that might be struggling in certain subjects. Whether you charge an hourly rate or a fixed cost, a homework helper will always be profitable. Leverage Facebook to message parents if you can set up a time to start helping their kids with homework.

IDEA NO. 59

Young Entrepreneurs Club

Have a passion for entrepreneurship? Start a club around entrepreneurship and charge them a fee to join.

The key is to provide a ton of value in this group to make it worth joining. Market your group on social media to find new group members that are willing to join.

IDEA NO. 60

Videographer

Love recording? A Videographer is an excellent job to show off your creativity and earn some income. One way to earn passive income as a videographer is by setting up courses as an evergreen product to sell online.

Leverage social media to showcase your work and use Instagram DM's to reach out to smaller content creators and artists if they need any help with recording.

IDEA NO. 61

Delivery Bakery

Love baking? Start a delivery service that provides fresh goods right at people's doors.

Social media will be your best friend since all the orders will be coming online. Take pictures of your tasty goods and use social media for marketing yourself to your target audience.

IDEA NO. 62

Powerwashing

Love satisfying jobs? A power washing business could be right up your alley. Spread the word locally by using before and after photos of sidewalks, driveways, and patios.

Power Washing is constantly in demand. The best way to promote this type of business is by showing tangible results!

IDEA NO. 63

Handyman

Are you handy around your house? Use those skills to build a handyman business that does the odd jobs that no one else knows how to do!

Are you worried about demand? Don't be; a good handyman is constantly booked up through word-of-mouth referrals.

IDEA NO. 64

Gardening Services

Love working with plants and flowers? Put a Facebook post out that you are willing to help plant flowers, bushes, and miniature trees. You can perform many tasks, including watering, trimming, digging, planting, and leaf-blowing, to keep your customer's homes and yards beautiful.

If you feel inclined, go an extra length and add mulching and weeding to your list of services.

IDEA NO. 65

Resume Expert

Everyone needs a job these days. An impressive resume is crucial to landing that dream job. Study up how to create the perfect resume through watching YouTube videos and consulting professionals.

Once you have figured out how to create an excellent resume, start selling your services to those looking to land their IDEA NO.1 job in a particular industry.

IDEA NO. 66

Extreme Couponer

Love free stuff? Learn how to 'extreme coupon' and get all the latest deals on hot products and resell them online for a higher amount.

There are tons of resourceful blogs and websites on saving tons of money at big box stores.

IDEA NO. 67

Cat Sitter

Are you a cat person? Offer cat sitting services to locals for when they go away on vacation.

You work on your own term and accept bookings based on your profitability and when you want to work.

IDEA NO. 68

Laundry Business

Everyone needs their laundry done, but so many despise laundry or simply don't have the time to do it. Start a business where you can handle your customers' laundry for them!

Although the IDEA NO. may seem silly, this business would thrive in populated areas where you have multiple clients in one area.

IDEA NO. 69

Rental Company

Have some upfront investment capital? Invest in some bouncy houses and start renting them out for a flat fee.

Make sure to factor in the time it takes to deliver, set up, and take down each bouncy house!

IDEA NO. 70

Car Washing Business

Who doesn't love a clean car? Start a car washing business that comes to you. People will be much more likely to get their car washed when it's in their own driveway.

Consider expanding and pairing this with a detailing business, and you could make some serious dough!

IDEA NO. 71

Ghostwriter

Are you an excellent writer but aren't interested in writing your own book or articles? Ghostwriters are constantly in demand for celebrity books, articles, and so much more.

Once you have a few gigs under your belt, create a portfolio to use when pitching future clients. You can use online platforms like Fiverr and Upwork to gain experience.

IDEA NO. 72

Scrapbooker

Into scrapbooking? Create a business where people can drop off their photos for you to turn them into a beautiful scrapbook!

This is extremely popular for baby and wedding photos, so make sure to focus your advertising on these two industries.

IDEA NO. 73

Phone Case Business

Selling phone cases can be lucrative as the margins are enormous. Find or create a unique phone case style and create a brand with a message behind it.

Although there's an excess of phone case companies, you could be golden if you create something unique with a strong intended message behind it.

IDEA NO. 74

Custom Shoe Painting

Custom shoes are big business and getting bigger every year. People of all kinds will pay up for one-of-a-kind, hand-painted custom shoes. While your first few pairs of custom kicks probably won't sell for thousands of dollars, you'll probably still be able to turn a modest profit.

A great way to grow your social media is to create a community using hashtags relevant to what you do. Once you get the business running, these eye-catching shoes will grab people's attention fast!

IDEA NO. 75

Photo Booth Rental

Photo booths are always hot items at parties. Consider purchasing all the necessary supplies for your own photo booth and rent it out to party-goers.

Once you make back your initial investment, the rest is all profit.

IDEA NO. 76

Furniture Assembly

Love building different kinds of stuff? Start a service online where people can request you to help build their equipment.

You only need some tools for start-up costs besides just following directions, and you can start getting paid immediately.

IDEA NO. 77

Driveway Sealcoating

Live in a populated town? A driveway seal coating business is a high-demand service that can be very profitable.

Start marketing your service on social media such as Facebook and target the right audience in your area. Join Facebook groups in your area and take before and after pictures of your work, and finding clients will be no problem.

IDEA NO. 78

Email Management

No one likes organizing all their emails, so being an email manager is a great way to lift some stress off of someone's shoulders and get paid.

You'll be surprised how many emails smaller businesses and content creators get. Start messaging them through Instagram and see if you can offer your service for a fee.

IDEA NO. 79

Auto Services On-The-Go

Are you a car fanatic and love fast cars and know everything about them? Start a repair shop to fix cars in your area on the go.

Once you master how all the car parts work on the back of your hand, you can start making money instantly.

IDEA NO. 80

Niche Websites

Passionate about a topic? Create a niche website on a topic you're interested in and start getting paid.

By writing content on the website every day, you can sell ads and affiliate links to customers. Eventually, you can build an email list and sell your own products.

IDEA NO. 81

Self-Publish a Book

Love writing? Creating a book can be very profitable if you know how to market yourself well.

Social media will be your best friend to showcase your book on all platforms and have a high SEO ranking so customers can find you easily.

IDEA NO. 82

Clothing Rental

Have lots of clothes and are a little tight on budget? Start renting them out online for some extra cash. You can rent out items for up to one week and charge a certain percentage of the rental price as the fee. The fee covers the service charges, dry cleaning, and other minor expenditures.

Leverage your website for sales and use social media for marketing your products and finding new customers.

IDEA NO. 83

Virtual Thrift Store

Have too many clothes and don't know what to do with them? Starting your own virtual thrift store is an excellent gig for you.

Making content around your store on social media such as Tik Tok will give you a boost in sales and help with brand exposure.

IDEA NO. 84

Door Hangers

Starting a door hanger business is an excellent way to get instant eyes on your service or product.

Once you master designing and printing the door hangers, reach out to smaller businesses in your area and social media and explain why having a door hanger for their product is beneficial.

IDEA NO. 85

Lead Generator

Do you think you're a people person? Become a lead generator and help other companies increase their sales.

Once you find your niche, create a website and figure out what leads you want to generate to convert those customers to other businesses.

IDEA NO. 86

Food Stand

Are you an incredible chef and want to earn some extra cash as a part-timer? Create a food stand around the corner to rack up some cash.

Choose the area carefully as populated areas with few restaurants can increase your sales. Once you gather all your ingredients and equipment, you can start selling. Leverage social media to create content with your food to generate more customers.

IDEA NO. 87

Media Company

Wanna control the news? Pick a niche that you're passionate about and start writing content around it. For starters, you can work from home and convert it into a proper business once you have gained enough experience.

Building a media company isn't easy. You have to be making content every day on all the platforms and have a clear vision of where you want to go in the future.

IDEA NO. 88

Pinterest Expert

Know everything about Pinterest? Help out other businesses by being a Pinterest expert.

Use your expertise in running ad campaigns for other businesses and showing off your social media work to maximize the number of potential customers.

IDEA NO. 89

Ice Cream Stand

Are you bored on a hot sunny day? Create an ice cream stand near some of your local sports games around your area.

Creating an ice cream stand doesn't cost much and can be very profitable when camping outside sports games.

IDEA NO. 90

Garden Designer

Turning your green-fingered hobby into a full-time career could be easier than you may think. You can become a sought-after specialist who helps families, businesses, and organisations turn their green spaces into beautiful, functional, and rewarding places to spend their time.

Leverage social media to show off your past designs to find new customers.

IDEA NO. 91

Party Organizer

Are you a party animal? You can organize parties for a living by starting your own party organizer business as party planning is always in demand.

This is an excellent option for someone who is organized, good at budgeting, and loves to have fun!

IDEA NO. 92

Translator

Do you speak multiple languages? Start a translator business. You can be an in-person translator as well as a virtual translator.

If this hustle suits you and you can build your reputation as a professional translator, you may even be able to travel for free as a perk of this business!

IDEA NO. 93

Specialty Drinks

Specialty drinks are in! Start a specialty drinks business that sells coffee-related products.

With this type of business, you need to stay up to date with the latest trends constantly.

IDEA NO. 94

Tour Guide

Do you live in a tourist hot spot and know everything about your town? Start a tour guide business where clients can hire you to guide them around your city.

Informational tours can be a profitable business, and they aren't highly price-sensitive services. You can build your reputation using online platforms and reach your potential audience.

IDEA NO. 95

Yoga Instructor

Are you into yoga? Master everything yoga-related and then teach classes of your own. Not just because there are bills to pay, but because a healthy income leads to a healthy life.

Find a local gym to partner with and split the profits for your classes.

IDEA NO. 96

Niche Pages

Love social media? Consider starting a niche page that focuses on posting content around a specific topic.

Make sure you choose a niche around something you are passionate about so you genuinely enjoy making/finding content around the topic.

IDEA NO. 97

Podcast

Grab a few of your friends and start a podcast where you talk about a particular set of topics. You need to know your targeted audience and some good knowledge about the topics you are discussing.

Try not to talk about anything and everything, as you will struggle to gain consistent viewers.

IDEA NO. 98

Nutrition Coach

Knowledgeable on nutrition? Become a nutrition coach and train others on how to be healthier.

If you don't want to train others directly, consider starting a YouTube channel surrounding nutrition in general. Use affiliate links to monetize!

IDEA NO. 99

Life Coach

Have you changed your life around for the better? Use your story and mindset tactics to coach others on how to prosper in life.

Being a life coach is extremely rewarding, especially when you truly help change your clients' lives. Once you build your reputation, you can earn a hefty amount from your experience.

IDEA NO. 100

Paparazzi

Love drama and live in the right area? Become a paparazzi.

Paparazzi connected to creators and celebrities are making a fortune off simply capturing interesting content and posting it to their YouTube channels.

IDEA NO. 101

Window Cleaning

Not afraid of heights? Give window cleaning a shot. Window cleaning is constantly in need and is a tedious job many homeowners are willing to outsource. The beauty of starting a window cleaning business is that you start making money right now.

Take before and after photos and market your services online!

IDEA NO. 102

Reselling Cards

Do you love sports cards? The Sports Card Market is nuts. Study up how to understand the value of these cards and build up a collection by buying and selling to earn a profit.

There are tons of online videos that share valuable insights on reselling cards.

IDEA NO. 103

Carpet Cleaning

If you have a few thousand dollars to invest, consider purchasing a heavy-duty carpet cleaner. Once you earn back your initial investment, everything else is profit!

Carpet cleaning is constantly in demand, especially with landlords. Try to connect with some landlords who own a massive apartment complex and strike a deal where you can get the job every time someone moves out.

IDEA NO. 104

Computer Repair

Let's be real. Computers are constantly breaking, getting viruses or freezing. Use your tech skills to start a computer repair business.

If this industry is already saturated near you, offer some unique services that will make you stand out, for example, 24 hour "guaranteed repair or it's free!".

IDEA NO. 105

Modeling

Like being a star? Start your modeling career modeling by taking pictures of yourself and posting them on social media.

Once you build your portfolio, reach out to modeling agencies to take you on and start shooting to earn money. You can even become a beauty influencer using online platforms like Instagram.

IDEA NO. 106

Handmade Jewelry

Love jewelry? Start your own jewelry business at home! Making your own jewelry is an excellent business to start because it doesn't have much start-up cost.

Use social media to show off your products and build brand awareness to drive sales.

IDEA NO. 107

Pet Grooming

Love animals? Start a service around your area that grooms pets. At the most basic level, you can make money by charging different rates for various services that can include haircut, bath, facial, etc.

Market your service on Facebook by targeting the right audience through running ads in your area.

IDEA NO. 108

Mobile Repair

Let's be honest everyone cracked their phone at least once or had phone problems. Start a service to repair phones that might be damaged.

Once you are knowledgeable about how to fix a phone properly, you can start building your brand awareness on social media in your area. You can create a website where people can easily schedule a time to drop off their phones for you to fix them.

IDEA NO. 109

Knitting Club

Do you like knitting? Show people in your area how to knit by creating a knitting club and charging them a fee.

By building a brand on social media, you can target the right audience through your club advertisements. Post 'how to' videos on YouTube and create a subscription-based service for exclusive content for your loyal supporters.

IDEA NO. 110

Soap and Lotion Kits

Let's face it; everyone wants to smell good. By Selling homemade soap and lotion kits online, you can make some serious money. You can use your creativity to make unique products with customized shapes and scents.

Leverage social media such as TikTok by creating content around your products and showcasing them to potential customers.

IDEA NO. 111

Flea Market Vendor

Want to sell some unique stuff? Be a vendor at your local flea market and earn a quick buck. Once you found the flea market, you want to sell at, set up a booth and start advertising your products.

The amount you can expect to bring in per weekend or day depends on your location and the type of merchandise you're selling.

IDEA NO. 112

Gutter Cleaner

Want to get your hands dirty? Start a service where you can clean other people's gutters in your area.

Leverage Facebook to find potential customers when running your service through ads by targeting older audiences.

IDEA NO. 113

Bicycle Repair

A mechanically inclined entrepreneur interested in cycling can earn a great income repairing bicycles right from the comfort of a home-based workshop. Create a business model around you repairing other bikes. You can choose to offer tune-ups for a flat fee and charge more for additional repairs.

Set up shop in your garage and market your brand on social media, so your area is well known for your service.

IDEA NO. 114

Dance Instructor

Do you like dancing and want to make some extra cash? Become a dance instructor to help others learn your moves. No matter what type of student you teach or what community you serve, better instructors will attract more students, more money, and ultimately, more profits.

Being a dance instructor might be a little tedious at the beginning for younger kids. Still, it'll pay off by expressing your love for the sport to the younger generation.

IDEA NO. 115

Makeup Service

Like doing makeup? Become a makeup stylus in your area.

Becoming a makeup stylus is a great way to show off your creativity and talents to your customers. Document your journey and take pictures of your finished customer makeup look on social media.

IDEA NO. 116

Publication

Like writing? Being a publication is a great way to get out your thoughts and document

someone else's new ventures. Switching to digital can also help you cut costs and increase your magazine's revenue.

Once you pick a niche, create a website and start writing relevant news about that niche.

IDEA NO. 117

Talent Manager

Do you want a tap into the entertainment industry? Become a talent manager and manage the top talents.

Remember, being a talent manager isn't easy. You're going to need experience and good communication skills to consistently advance your talents to the next level.

IDEA NO. 118

Author

Being an author is a great way to showcase your experience and creativity to help impact the world in a certain way. You can become a self-published author and earn up to 70% royalties from your books.

You can write the best boo,k but you won't get any sales if you can't market your product properly. Using social media and SEO ranking is your best bet.

IDEA NO. 119

Accessory Shop

Creating an accessory store is a great way to earn some extra cash and sell products you're passionate about.

Once you pick the niche you want to target, having a professional website and marketing your products on social media will help you in the long run.

IDEA NO. 120

Shopify Store Creator

Are you an expert at creating profitable Shopify dropshipping stores? Consider building out stores and selling them to entrepreneurs looking for passive income.

Take care of the niche research, web design and execution to prove the potential success of your store.

IDEA NO. 121

Digital Products

If you are looking to make passive income. Consider creating a line of digital products that will be sold over and over again. You can offer various possibilities from domain name and hosting to web design, e-marketing and Search Engine Optimization.

Create high-value products and aim to sell lots of them with an expert marketing strategy.

IDEA NO. 122

Course

Are you an expert in a highly desirable industry? Create a course that teaches a step by step process of implementing your tips and tricks to become successful in that specific industry.

Courses are one of the most popular and profitable digital products as of now. You can even sell your courses on online platforms like Udemy and Coursera.

IDEA NO. 123

Slideshow Expert

Expert at making PowerPoints? Everyday tons and tons of presentations are shared in every type of business. Study how to create the best pitch decks and presentations and turn them into a business.

You may want to create tier pricing where higher tiers have upgraded graphics and more attention to detail for a business like this. You can sell your services online too on platforms like Fiverr and Upwork

IDEA NO. 124

Dog Trainer

Adore dogs and know how to control and train one? Turn this into money by helping dog owners with rowdy pets.

Dog trainers can make a fortune, especially when your results are extremely evident!

IDEA NO. 125

Lip Balm Shop

Love lip balms? Start creating your own products. Purchase bulk tubes and materials and design your packaging to get started! You can even make customized orders for higher rates.

This could be a fun business, especially if you have a mission behind it, such as "for each lip balm sold, 10% of proceeds go to help to plant trees".

IDEA NO. 126

Pool Maintenance

Have extra time in the summer? Start a pool maintenance company that offers weekly pool cleaning services. You can visit client's homes or businesses to check and adjust the water's chemical balance, maintain the pumps and filters, check the skimmers, and clean.

If you can get enough clients and stay busy, you are golden!

IDEA NO. 127

Party Set-up

Enjoy party planning? Help clients execute their planning by helping them set up the food, tables, chairs and everything else that makes a party awesome.

This is a rewarding business as it helps take the stress off your clients.

IDEA NO. 128

Email Manager

Are you a professional when it comes to answering emails? Find clients that are willing to outsource some of their email checkings to you.

Of course, they will still have to respond to some emails personally. Still, if you can organize what's junk and what's important, this will help them prioritize their time.

IDEA NO. 129

Banner Business

Do you know how to create animated graphics? You can make a pretty penny for doing this for a living!

Whether you are doing this for companies and designing ads or for YouTubers looking for an updated intro video, make sure you have a strong portfolio that shows off the quality of your work!

IDEA NO. 130

eBay Seller

Have a lot of old stuff around the house and want to make an extra buck? Start selling some products on eBay.

Once you've gained some experience selling some of your old stuff and want to expand, start looking into thrift stores and garage sales to find products to flip.

IDEA NO. 131

Holiday Decorator

Love holidays? Create a service where you decorate people's houses in your area.

Market yourself on social media such as Facebook to target the right audience. Take pictures of your work and showcase them to potential customers online.

IDEA NO. 132

Instagram Consultant

Social media is only becoming more popular. Start helping smaller businesses expand their brand online by being an Instagram consultant.

Reach out to smaller businesses on Instagram that lack a social media presence and provide them with a value for a fee.

IDEA NO. 133

Virtual Assistant

If you're good at staying organized, help someone out and become a virtual assistant. You can work remotely and make money from the comfort of your home. There is no limit to what you can do because there is a large variety of work available.

Let other people know about your service on social media and connect with potential customers on LinkedIn.

IDEA NO. 134

Computer Training

If you are a tech-savvy person in the modern world, you know that information technology is the place to be when you want to find a sweet gig with great pay. Create a course for beginners on how to operate computers and teach them about programs such as excel.

Start marketing your service on social media to find potential customers.

IDEA NO. 135

Handmade Pottery

Like pottery? Start your own pottery business at your house. Creating your niche is the first step to really creating the pottery you want to make. The best way to do it is through research and figure out how much effort you'll need to put into it.

Create content around your finished products and showcase them to potential customers on social media.

IDEA NO. 136

Video Animator

Like animation? Start creating animations online for businesses and content creators. You can even make a short, upload it to

YouTube, monetize your channel by enabling ads and watch the money flows.

Start marketing your service on social media such as LinkedIn and use platforms like Fiverr and Upwork to get a potential gig.

IDEA NO. 137

Fishing Boat Rides

Like fishing and having a boat? Start a business where you take people out on fishing trips and show them how to cast and catch the best fish. You can even rent out your boat to earn some extra cash.

Showcase and market your business on social platforms.

IDEA NO. 138

Food Truck

Like cooking? Chef up some food in a truck and start selling them in your area. The business does not require a lot of investment, and you can make lots of money if you know the market well.

Document your journey on social media and use hashtags that are relevant to your niche and area.

IDEA NO. 139

Housekeeper

Like cleaning? Become a housekeeper for someone else.

Offer your service to the people in need online and have a website so your potential customers can book you.

IDEA NO. 140

Haircuts

Like cutting hair, and you are good at it? Become a hairstylist by setting up a shop in your house. You can do it part-time in the beginning. As you gain some experience in it, you can raise your rates and open your own salon.

Once you get your hairstylist certificate, you can approach potential customers through online platforms.

IDEA NO. 141

Magician

Like magic tricks? Become a magician and show off your creativity and skills to the world. You can start doing small shows at schools or birthday parties and expand the business after getting experience.

Start recording videos of you doing your magic tricks and drive potential customers to your website, where you can get bookings for parties and events.

IDEA NO. 142

Soccer Trainer

If you are a soccer fan and are good at it? Become a trainer and start your own set-up where you showcase your talents and teach other kids how to play Soccer.

Start private lessons in your area and use social media to showcase your skills by running ads to potential customers.

IDEA NO. 143

On-The-Go Nail Service

Let's face it, every person wants to look good. Becoming a nail stylist is a great way to earn some extra cash and provide confidence to customers.

Take pictures of your clients that have used your service and showcase your excellent work on the Internet to kickstart your whole business.

IDEA NO. 144

Meditation Instructor

If you are one of the people whose life has been changed by meditation, it is the right gig for you. Use your experience and skills to create a service where you teach others how to meditate.

Having a social media presence to showcase your work and your brand will get more leads to your service. Use Facebook to target people in your area.

IDEA NO. 145

Affiliate Marketer

Intrigued by affiliate marketing? Do your research and find some products in a profitable niche and start earning right away!

Make sure to vet the products you promote to ensure they are of good quality!

IDEA NO. 146

Computer Programming

Are you a computer genius? Start a computer programming business where you help others learn computer language and coding. You can even sell your courses on online platforms like Udemy and Coursera to earn some passive income.

Although computer programming is by no means easy, once you learn it, you can make some serious money.

IDEA NO. 147

Staging Rentals

Have some start-up funds? Consider starting a prop rental business where you come and add props to homes before getting for sale photos taken!

Build up a small inventory to start, and as you become more popular, continue to expand.

IDEA NO. 148

Phone Charging Station

Purchase a phone charging station that you can put some coins in and charge your phone. Reach out to local businesses regarding placing them in their stores.

Although you most likely won't make a full-time income from this business, it can be a great side hustle!

IDEA NO. 149

Sanitizing Business

Germs are everywhere. Start a business that provides sanitizing services for different places such as your house, cars, or office. It will require only a little investment, and if you stay professional, you can earn big in the long run.

Consider creating a subscription style business where they subscribe and receive your services weekly or monthly.

IDEA NO. 150

Iced Coffee Stand

Everyone loves coffee, and people want it in different forms. Iced coffee is especially popular among kids and is a bit more expensive than normal coffee. Get creative with an iced coffee stand and take advantage of this fact. This gig will be a refreshing hit on a hot day.

Use social media to expand your business and gain loyal customers.

IDEA NO. 151

Swing Set Company

Every other house has a swing set in their backyard! Someone needs to assemble all these massive playgrounds! Start a swing set assembly company that charges a flat rate per assembly.

Make sure to grab some friends as this is a big job and won't be possible without a crew.

IDEA NO. 152

Message Manager

Know a celebrity or public figure that can't handle all their direct messages? Start a message manager business where you handle their accounts and respond to the various inquiries they get.

Believe it or not, most celebrities have multiple people helping run their accounts.

IDEA NO. 153

Shaved Ice Business

Love shaved ice? Head over to the local baseball field and set up shop with your shaved ice materials.

Create some appealing signage, and don't forget your tip jar.

IDEA NO. 154
Beach Crew

Live near a beach? Consider helping out families deliver and set up their beach equipment to make their vacation a bit more relaxing. You can even provide lifeguard services to earn some extra cash.

Do an over the top amazing job, and word of mouth will spread rapidly.

IDEA NO. 155
Fire Pit Set up

People love their fire pits. Start a company that goes to people's houses and assembles a firepit for a set rate. You can earn some hefty money through this gig if your location is good and it's freezing out there.

Add in extras such as wood delivery, fire starters and much more to earn as much money as possible.

IDEA NO. 156

Water Bottle Business

Create a reusable water bottle business with a positive message behind it that you genuinely believe in. You can create different designs and sizes to attract customers of every age.

Everyone uses water bottles, and word of mouth spreads quickly when a new popular water bottle brand is in town!

IDEA NO. 157

Shoelace Business

Are you a sneakerhead? Create custom shoelaces to match some of the hottest kicks.

You can customize the length, color, size, etc., of your laces to match different demands from potential customers.

Going to sneaker conventions is a great way to initially get your business name out there!

IDEA NO. 158

Book Marketing

The biggest part about launching a successful book is marketing it. Study exactly how to successfully launch a self-published book and then create your business, helping others do the same.

Books are everywhere. If your service is effective, it is bound to be a successful company.

IDEA NO. 159

Bulk Buying

Start a business that buys things in bulk and resells them for cheaper. Try to find items that are needed over and over again so you can have repeated customers.

For example, buying paper products such as paper plates and bowls that get shipped right to your door could be a great model as they run out easily.

IDEA NO. 160

Personalized Chef

Like cooking? Become a personal chef and teach others how to cook. You can provide your services online as well as in person. Create courses and sell them to online platforms like Coursera and Udemy.

Start showcasing your recipes online and build an audience so you can start advertising your cookbooks, merch and Brand deals etc.

IDEA NO. 161

Birthday Party Character

Love entertaining kids? Every child has a favorite character, princess or superhero that can be incorporated into a party. Show off your goofy side and become a birthday party character.

Advertise your service on Facebook to potential clients and create a website so people can book you.

IDEA NO. 162

Balloon Artist

Show off your creativity and entertain kids by being a balloon artist. Remember that balloon artist are in the business of entertaining. It is more important how good of an entertainer you are than how impressive your balloon art is.

Start shooting videos and posting on social media to attract more potential customers to book you for events.

IDEA NO. 163

Elder Sitter

Like helping people? Become an elder sitter for the people in need. You can provide companionship and non-medical care to senior citizens. You can assist your clients with their everyday activities and errands, such as grocery shopping, cooking, cleaning, and traveling to appointments or leisure activities.

Let families around your area know your availability and set up times where you can book and track your days.

IDEA NO. 164

Windshield Repair Service

Let's be real. Window fixing is a pain and can be tedious for many people. Use your skills to start a business where you repair windows.

Do something unique if this market is too saturated in your area. Leverage social media and SEO rankings to boost your business.

IDEA NO. 165

Facebook Ads Strategist

If you're an expert with Facebook, become a Facebook ad strategist by creating your own service and offering help to other businesses.

Having a portfolio of your results and reaching out to businesses through DM's will give you a high chance of closing your first client.

IDEA NO. 166

Music Accessory Business

Music culture is one of the biggest things around the world. Do you know anyone who doesn't enjoy music? Start a music accessory business that provides unique earphones with custom designs and color schemes.

Accessories seem like small businesses, but they rake in billions of dollars annually as people's love for music evolves.

IDEA NO. 167

Snowboarding Instructor

Do you enjoy snowboarding and are actually good at it? Create a business model where you become a snowboard instructor by teaching your skills to others.

Start with private lessons and slowly expand by adding more people to your groups. Use social media to leverage your service and take pictures and videos of your work.

IDEA NO. 168

Golf-Club Cleaning

Golfers spend considerable amounts of money on the best equipment they can. You can leverage this opportunity and use your free time to earn some extra cash. Create a service where you clean others' golf clubs at your local country clubs.

Advertise your service on Facebook and offer your service at local country clubs, and you'll get great tips.

IDEA NO. 169

Lacrosse Stringing

Let's face it, every lacrosse player wants the best stick. Create a business where you string across heads in your area.

Use social media to leverage your service and talents. All you need is one viral video in your area. And word-of-mouth spread quickly.

IDEA NO. 170

Custom Jerseys

Love sports? Create a business where you redesign jerseys and customize them for profit. You can target different designs to attract more customers, for example, soccer, anime, movies, etc.

Use TikTok to show off your brand and make video content around your jerseys. A lot of people enjoy watching the process of starting a business and designing.

IDEA NO. 171

Henna Artist

Like art? Become a henna designer by expressing your artistic skills on one's skin.

By using social media by taking pictures of your work and expressing them to others, you'll slowly start to build supporters that will pay for your service.

IDEA NO. 172

Custom Shoes

Are you a sneakerhead? Start a business where you customize sneakers.

Reach out to top creators in the industry by giving them free pairs of your customers shoes in exchange for a shout out. This will help build your brand and get more eyes on your page where you show your products.

IDEA NO. 173

Surf Instructor

Do you love adventure and are good at surfing? Become a surf instructor for the local beach. You can make a hefty amount at camps and substantially more via private lessons.

Advertise and document your journey on social media to get potential leads and kickstart your service by having private lessons.

IDEA NO. 174

Creative Vending Machine Business

Start a vending machine business that doesn't have your typical items. Whether this carries earphones and protein powder at the gym or PPE at a hospital, think outside of the box.

It can get your vending machine more attention, especially when your products are specifically meant for the area where the machine is placed.

IDEA NO. 175

Framed Quotes

Create an Etsy shop selling framed quotes from well-known celebrities, activists and politicians.

Promote your shop through your social profiles and showcase your products in action!

IDEA NO. 176

Drone Photography

Into photography and want to earn as a part-timer? Purchase a drone and offer drone photography for real estate agents in the area.

Approach local real estate agents with flyers showcasing your work! Make sure to follow all local drone laws and regulations.

IDEA NO. 177

Hat Patches

Create a hat business that has an interchangeable patch in the front that attaches via velcro.

This way, your customers can buy a single hat and an array of various customized patches to create a unique product.

IDEA NO. 178

Shrub Trimming

Start a business that offers shrub trimming for locals. Most big companies don't want small jobs, so there will be tons of work for you.

Market your business using before and after photos in local neighborhood groups. Also, consider leaving flyers in your neighbourhood.

IDEA NO. 179

Airbrush Shirts

Are you into art and want to learn a new skill? Watch some online tutorials and invest in blank shirts and an airbrush machine.

These businesses do extremely well when you set up a booth at softball or baseball tournaments. If there are none in your area, consider coming to a vendor at different high traffic events.

IDEA NO. 180

Amazon Affiliate Site

Start an affiliate site that shows some of the best Amazon deals for a specific niche. Users will purchase the product through your link on Amazon, and you will receive a small commission.

These sites are easy to set up and can earn passive income over time. Get creative on how to drive traffic to your site.

IDEA NO. 181

SEO Expert

Ever wonder how something ranks on the first page of a search engine? This is called search engine optimization (commonly referred to as SEO). Study up on what it takes to have your website rank high on Google and then help others improve their SEO ranking.

SEO is an extremely important thing for businesses that rely on Google searches as their main traffic source.

IDEA NO. 182

Drama Channel

Start a YouTube channel or social media page that covers a celebrity drama. Pages like this can blow up quickly due to their quick reporting and interest surrounding drama.

Firstly, build up a strong audience and monetize later on by selling advertisements against your followers.

IDEA NO. 183

Audio Book Reader

Audiobook companies are constantly looking for freelancers willing to read audiobooks and have their voices recorded.

Do you have an intriguing voice? This could be for you!

IDEA NO. 184

Pizza Delivery Company

Start a pizza delivery company where all local pizza shops can outsource all their deliveries to you cheaper than hiring a full-time delivery person.

Create a website or mobile app that connects your business with pizzerias in your area.

IDEA NO. 185

Home Tech

Start a home tech company that comes to your house and analyzes your current technology, and explains what can be improved to save you money over time.

For example: encouraging homeowners to swap out their current light bulbs with LED bulbs will help them save a fortune on their electricity bill.

IDEA NO. 186

Linkedin Optimization

Linkedin is the ultimate job finding platform. Start a business that helps users optimize their Linkedin profile to the best shot at getting hired!

This may seem over the top, but a professional-looking Linkedin profile could make or break a job application.

IDEA NO. 187

Low Content Books

Want to publish a book but have been struggling to write that perfect manuscript? Writing low-content books offer a simple way for almost anyone to become a published author – with very little writing skill required.

Start a business surrounding low content books. Find untapped but in-demand niches and create books that will earn you passive income over time.

IDEA NO. 188

Game With Me

Start an online service that connects like-minded individuals to play video games together.

Although the service is most likely free, monetize the site with advertisements and affiliate links.

IDEA NO. 189

Toy Review Channel

One of the most profitable niches on YouTube is creating a toy review page.

Once you learn how to edit or outsource your editing, start unboxing and reviewing the new hottest toys on the Internet.

IDEA NO. 190

Customized Products

Like doodling? Start a business where you start customizing products by using your creative art skills. The best thing about this gig is you can doodle any object – you are not restricted to one niche.

Create a website and start showcasing your products on social media to get potential customers.

IDEA NO. 191

SAT/College Prep Tutor

Did you score high on the SAT and love helping others with your knowledge? Start teaching other students with their exams by tutoring them, either online or in person.

Many parents would favor someone that just took the SAT rather than having a 45-year-old person tutor their kids. Use social media to leverage your service.

IDEA NO. 192

Cake Decorator

Love baking? Got an eye for frosting details? Show off your creativity by being a cake decorator for special events. You can set a rule to charge 250% of the ingredient costs.

Be unique with it by creating wild designs and use social media to show off your cakes.

IDEA NO. 193

Dog Toys

Love dogs? Use your creative IDEA NO.s and make fun toys for pets. You can take help from the internet to make toys from household items. You can make a tennis rope or a DIY tennis ball, etc.

Leverage social media and try to start trends with your products for the best results.

IDEA NO. 194

Reusable Straw Business

Start a business that sells reusable straws to do your part in creating environmental impact. Straws can easily slip through recycling machines and end up in oceans for decades.

Creating this business will not only be fulfilling in that you are doing a good deed for the environment, but it can also be profitable as there is a huge demand for products in this niche.

IDEA NO. 195

Tie-Dye Business

A tie-dye business is an excellent IDEA NO. because you have a wide range of products you can choose to tie-dye through shoes, tablecloths or clothes.

The tie-dye market is in high demand, so you can attract future customers online by taking pictures and videos of your products. Use TikTok to market your content and get potential sales.

IDEA NO. 196

Art Classes

Think you're a good artist? Start using your skills and teach younger kids how to draw. You can diversify your income and build meaningful connections with others.

You can start private lessons, give live workshops or tutorials on YouTube and make money from AdSense.

IDEA NO. 197

Flag Business

Let's face it, every college student has some sort of flag in their dorm. Start a business where you design unique flags for college students. You will need to decide on the framework for your operation and invest in buying the required equipment.

Leverage social media by posting Memes and funny college clips to help get more creative IDEA NO.s about your business.

IDEA NO. 198

eBook

Are you an expert at something? Start selling your knowledge through e-books that can bring value to some people.

Leverage your book through big niche pages and influencers in your niche to drive sales to your website.

IDEA NO. 199

Lip Gloss Business

Start a lip gloss business by expanding your brand on social media. Starting a lip gloss business is fast and easy, as you don't need an investor or some special knowledge. You can take customized orders to make your service unique.

You want to be showcasing your products and the process of making your homemade lip gloss by taking videos and posting them.

IDEA NO. 200

Landing Page Specialist

If you love designing and writing, becoming a landing page specialist is for you. Regardless of what you're doing online to make money, a landing page is going to be the solid choice for overrating money off the internet.

You can find your customers by listing your service on fiverr. Fiverr Is a great website to turn your skills into money and find your clients.

IDEA NO. 201

Wedding Photographer

Being a wedding photographer is one of the highest-paid positions in the photography field. Do not forget to check your sales agreement and the correct type of equipment required for every event.

This business can easily become a full-time career by making up to $10,000 per shoot.

IDEA NO. 202

LED lights

Create a business where you start programming your own led lights and selling them for profits.

Use the power of TikTok to create video content around your customized LED lights so younger kids will be more eager to buy them.

IDEA NO. 203

Reselling Electronics

Start collecting used electronics and build a business where you refurbish and resell them.

Start picking up used electronics through garage sales and Facebook marketplace to see if you can flip them on eBay.

IDEA NO. 204

Fill Out Online Surveys

Are you bored and want to earn some money? Start filling out online surveys as a side hustle.

You can start by filling out surveys through inbox dollars and survey Junkie to earn some money. Remember, this isn't gonna be a lot of money; thiswill is just a side hustle you can start when you're bored.

IDEA NO. 205

Template Creator

Interested in passive income? Create an array of different templates for niche items and sell them on Etsy.

Examples of this could be a business planner, fill in a blank calendar, and so much more.

IDEA NO. 206

Low Maintenance Website

Are you efficient in creating websites? Find a profitable niche and create a website that will maintain a strong ranking on Google over time.

Whether this is a tool, blog or service, create something that doesn't need to be updated often and earns you passive income through advertisements and affiliate links.

IDEA NO. 207

Job Pairing

Create a job pairing business that connects qualified candidates with jobs in their industry. You can take a commission from both sides after building a good reputation online.

Monetize this business by charging a subscription fee to the company or taking a transactional fee off their initial paycheck.

IDEA NO. 208

Bio-Link

Create a website that allows you to create a profile with different links and features. Users will place this link in their social media bio to promote their other social accounts and upcoming projects.

Make sure your domain name is short and catchy.

IDEA NO. 209

Outsourcing

Do you have good managing skills? You can outsource online or hire a freelancer to hire individuals to perform tasks online. You can work flexibility from home and this gig wouldn't require any major skills in a certain field.

Use social media to build your reputation and attract potential customers through it.

IDEA NO. 210

Sticker Company

Start a trendy sticker company that creates its own designs along and offers products for every age group. Once you have built your reputation, you can offer bulk orders to small businesses or organizations.

Stickers are an extremely popular product. Entice customers with a quick turnaround.

IDEA NO. 211

Memorabilia

Collectibles are items that usually fetch more money than they were originally worth. Start a business around them by buying and reselling different memorabilia online.

To ensure your business is successful, make sure to study and understand what will and will not be profitable.

IDEA NO. 212

Software Business

Are you a software geek or want to become one? Build useful software that will solve a problem in a specific industry.

This can be a profitable business, whether this is creating a sneaker software to ensure you secure the latest sneaker release or an email software that reduces spam!

IDEA NO. 213

Dream Job Program

Know what it takes to get your dream job? Create a program that gives users everything they need to get their dream job in their specific industry.

This course should contain digital products, including thank you letters, sample resumes and much more!

IDEA NO. 214

Video Tutors

Start a business connecting college students with younger students looking for a last-minute tutor through a web conference.

You can monetize this business by taking a service fee from each tutoring session.

IDEA NO. 215

Custom Music Plaque

Customizing unique music plates can be a high demand if you target the right people. Create a business where you put their favorite song on a glass plate that lights up.

Once you're all set up, start selling your products on Etsy to start earning income.

IDEA NO. 216

Sports Stickers

Create a business where you start selling stickers of your favorite sports players. You can make bumper stickers, bike stickers, boat stickers, motorcycle stickers, guitar stickers, etc.

Start off by marketing your products on social media and having a website so potential customers can buy your fat heads.

IDEA NO. 217

Stuffed Animals

Start a business where you make your own customizable stuffed animals for little kids. You can make these in different sizes and colors and attract many potential customers from your own area.

Use Tiktok and youtube to start making video content of your stuffed animals to turn your audience into income.

IDEA NO. 218

Handmade Pins

If you're already rocking pins on your clothing, you should create a business around it and start designing your own pins. Customize your service for people of different age groups to expand your business.

Create an Etsy shop selling your own customized pins.

IDEA NO. 219

Duct Tape Wallet

Use your creativity and start a business by making wallets and bags out of duct tape. This trend is especially popular among little kids. You can make your service unique by taking customized orders.

Leverage social media to show off your cool duct tape design wallets.

IDEA NO. 220

Pet Collars

Start a fashionable business by designing your own pet collars. You can outshine other businesses by making your collars durable, comfortable, and made of different materials for every customer.

Use Facebook ads to target people with pets in your area to kick start your business.

IDEA NO. 221

Mason Jars

Mason jars are being used for multiple purposes nowadays. Find a unique way to use your mason jars to attract potential customers and build a business around them. You can use creativity to make your jars beautiful & unique enough to make and sell at craft fairs and flea markets!

Use social media by taking pictures and videos of your Jars to build your brand.

IDEA NO. 222

Keychains & Lanyards

Start a keychain business where you design your own unique keychains by painting them. Make your own unique design or make customized orders to attract more customers.

Open your own Etsy shop with your customizable keys to start getting sales.

IDEA NO. 223

Homemade Chokers

Chokers are in. Pick up some material at your local craft store and design your homemade necklaces.

You can start offering your homemade Chokers on Etsy and eBay to kick start your business. Also, build a website to start funneling traffic to your store.

IDEA NO. 224

Pillow Business

Swapping out cushions is a great way to give a room a facelift without spending a fortune, so depending on where you're located, there might be quite a local market to tap into.

Document your pillow journey by showcasing how your homemade covers are created on social media. You need to develop a strong marketing plan for this business to become successful.

IDEA NO. 225

Computer Cases

Use your love for computers to design special cases for MacBooks.

Start directly selling your cases through eBay, Facebook, marketplace and even Etsy.

IDEA NO. 226

Headband Business

Headbands are in style. Start decorating and designing limited edition headbands for sports athletes.

Start giving out your headbands to content creators in the sports niche for free to boost your brand.

IDEA NO. 227

Console Skins

Use your creativity and love for gaming to build a business where you customize skins for consoles. If your IDEA NO.s are unique, you can sell them worldwide through platforms like Amazon.

Start making cool edits of your console skins online and use social media to directly target the gaming community.

IDEA NO. 228

Subscription Box Business

Build a subscription-based business model where you send out monthly gift boxes to your customers.

Once you pick your niche, you can directly target those groups of people on Facebook that might be interested in your gift boxes.

IDEA NO. 229

Wrapping Cars

Into cars? Build a service where you start wrapping customizing cars. Some legit companies will pay you for wrapping cars, including Carvertise, Free Car Media, and Wrapify.

If you want to get good exposure, Direct message bigger content creators to wrap their car for free.

IDEA NO. 230

Fitness Product

Are you a gym rat? Create a fitness product that will make working out easier for beginners.

The fitness industry is massive, and consumers are willing to spend lots of money to make their health.

IDEA NO. 231

Ring Business

Rings are for all genders. Create a handmade ring business that ships worldwide! Make unique products and take customized orders to expand your business.

Consider leveraging influencer marketing by sending some free products to influencers in exchange for promotion.

IDEA NO. 232

Coffee Delivery

Do all your neighbors run out to a local coffee shop every morning? Start a business that delivers their coffee straight to their front door for a small fee.

Consider trying to get multiple customers on the same block to make deliveries speedy.

IDEA NO. 233

Publisher

Learn the ropes of book marketing and start your own imprint by leveraging a print on demand service. Handle all the marketing for your client.

Take care of revisions, marketing, cover design and keyword SEO for your clients.

IDEA NO. 234

Android Games

Create a free android game that will earn you money through advertisements or affiliate links. Decide your niche, targeted gender and age group, and then proceed accordingly.

If you are not familiar with creating a game yourself, it's easy to find a freelancer who can help out!

IDEA NO. 235

Helmet Customizer

Love airbrushing? Create a business that customizes baseball and softball helmets with unique and eye-catching designs.

Create a website and social profiles to show off your portfolio of work.

IDEA NO. 236

Autopilot Video Site

Create an autopilot video site that shares free stock of relaxing videos such as fireplaces, raindrops or the ocean waves crashing to soothe people's minds and relieve them of their stress.

Monetize your website through advertisements, special offers and the option to subscribe for exclusive content.

IDEA NO. 237

Dog Bandanas

People love their pets. Start a dog bandana company that offers an array of different and unique designs.

If you think it would be beneficial, also offer custom designs for a higher price.

IDEA NO. 238

Sports Marketing Agency

Start an agency focused solely on helping connect athletes with brand deals. Now more than ever, athletes are looking for representation to profit from their name, image and likeness.

Start small and slowly expand your agency as you make more and more connections with brands looking to partner with your athletes.

IDEA NO. 239

Kid Camp

Start a small weekend camp where parents can sign up for an affordable rate to drop their kids off and be surprised by you and your friends.

Think babysitting but a few more babysitters and a few more kids. This will help make it a more affordable option for parents.

IDEA NO. 240

Talk Show

Start a talk show about something you are passionate about. Invite guests and build up a strong audience.

Money will come as your audience comes, but talk shows definitely don't grow overnight, so this hustle will require patience.

IDEA NO. 241

Video Doorbell Install

Video doorbells are becoming more and more common as technology improves. Start a doorbell install company that charges a flat fee to remove your old doorbell and install your new video doorbell.

This can be a great service-based business, especially in a highly-populated neighborhood.

IDEA NO. 242

Embroidery Business

Love custom branded clothing? Start an embroidery business where you take blank clothing and embroidery business logos for a set cost. You can earn a hefty amount through this business if you market it properly.

Custom clothing is a massive market, especially if you can have a quick turnaround.

IDEA NO. 243

Cookies That Come To You

Love baking? Start a cooking business that delivers cookies straight to your customer's door.

Make sure to follow all local health and safety guidelines when it comes to your business.

IDEA NO. 244

Fix Bikes

Are you knowledgeable about biking and, more importantly, how to fix a bike when it breaks? Start a company that helps repair broken bicycles.

Start off with basic repairs and expand as you have the space and capital for more equipment.

IDEA NO. 245

Handyperson

Do you think you can fix things? Become a handyman for your local area. You can charge based on the type of service requested, the number of hours needed, and the region in which you're requesting service.

Create a portfolio of the services you can provide to your customers.

IDEA NO. 246

Modded Controller

Use your expertise by creating modded controllers and selling them for a profit.

Show off your new controllers on social media and use eBay or even create your own website to display your products.

IDEA NO. 247

Haunted House

If you like scaring people, turn your home into a haunted house and charge people for their adventure.

Take videos of the experience and display them on social media to advertise your house.

IDEA NO. 248

Fish Tank Service

Cleaning fish tanks can be a tedious task. Offer a fish tank cleaning service that offers monthly packages to come and do the cleaning for them.

Once you know what you're doing, you can start running ads on social media for your service.

IDEA NO. 249

Airbnb Management Assistant

Help People who have Airbnb properties manage them prior to new renters arriving. Your responsibilities will include marketing their properties, growing reservations, and booking stays, as well as many of the day-to-day cleaning, stocking, and key exchange responsibilities.

Create a business plan and convince homeowners to hire you for your service.

IDEA NO. 250

Stuffed up Doll

Create your own doll business where you add unique decorations and sell them for a profit.

Leverage the Power of social media to advertise to the younger generation.

IDEA NO. 251

Clean Parking Lots

Starting a parking cleaning service is a good business to get yourself into with minimal start-up cost. You can benefit from commercial businesses in your area. At the same time, it can provide you with a lucrative opportunity to earn a good living by working for yourself.

Advertise your service through Facebook and make your work known around your community for the best results.

IDEA NO. 252

Collect Lost Golf Balls

There are usually thousands of golf balls in the lake or under trees. Start a business where you collect lost golf balls and resell them for a profit.

You can start making serious cash by selling your golf balls on eBay after cleaning them.

IDEA NO. 253

Pet Bakery

Do you love animals and baking? Start your own pet bakery where you sell dog treats to your customers. Startup costs are low, and You can run your business entirely as a home-based business.

Show off your treats on social media by taking pictures of them. Future customers will be attracted by your baking.

IDEA NO. 254

Pageant Sashes

Start sewing your own pageant sashes online by creating your own website.

Be unique with it by creating goofy designs or add patches to the sashes that represent certain things.

IDEA NO. 255

Cookie Dough Cafe

Let's face it, everyone loves eating raw cookie dough. Start making your own custom cookie dough café in your own kitchen.

People love seeing delicious foods on their socials. Start taking artsy pictures of your cookie dough to attract food lovers and potential customers. Make sure to follow all local health and safety guidelines when it comes to your business.

IDEA NO. 256

Treehouse Business

Create a business where you build mini tree houses for kids in your area. Many tree house companies operate with very little overhead. The largest ongoing expense will come from your marketing efforts.

Take pictures of your finished products and add them to your portfolio to show your future customers.

IDEA NO. 257

Boat Maintenance

If you live near the water, create a service to take care of boats by cleaning them.

Advertise your service on social media and start handing out flyers around your beach.

IDEA NO. 258

Alcohol Decor

Turn alcohol bottles into a profitable business by decorating them. For example, use a bottle to create a Fishtank and add custom designs on the outside.

You can start selling your products on Etsy and show off your bottles on TikTok to advertise to a new audience.

IDEA NO. 259

Dog Backpacks

Dog backpacks are in. Start creating your own business around a comfortable backpack that dogs can wear.

Make sure you design your backpacks that won't negatively affect the ability of dogs to walk and move.

IDEA NO. 260

Film Transfer Business

Interested in films and videos? Start a business that transfers old film into a digital copy.

Start locally, and when business takes off, consider starting an online store where customers can ship their film

IDEA NO. 261

Flower Planting

Love yard work? Start a flower planting business that delivers and plants flowers locally.

Make sure to study up on your knowledge of the different types of flowers and the best planting practices. Showcase your business using social media.

IDEA NO. 262

Paver Sand Installation

Lots of people have patios! Start a business that cleans out the weeds and betweens of paver stones and lays down a fresh coat of paver sand.

Although this can be tedious work, it can be satisfying once you see the end product.

IDEA NO. 263

Necklace Business

Are you a jewelry fanatic? Start a necklace business by gathering some materials and starting an online shop. It is a perfect venture for you if you wish to start part-time rather than quitting your current job and going all in.

Create meaningful packaging and a quality product, and you are good to go.

IDEA NO. 264

Custom Canvas

If you are obsessed with wall art, this may be for you! Create custom canvases and sell them online. Online shoppers are constantly looking for unique pieces to decorate their house with.

These could be paintings or digital art, whichever you prefer!

IDEA NO. 265

Party Favors

Start a business that allows busy parents to outsource customized party favors.

Take care of everything from A-Z in terms of unique party favors. Word of mouth will spread quickly at the party.

IDEA NO. 266

Professional Organizer

Are you extremely organized? Why not help others be more organized by starting a professional organizer business.

With a business like this, word of mouth will spread rapidly but also make sure to take before and after photos to build a portfolio of your work.

IDEA NO. 267

Driveway Sealing

Looking for some extra summer cash while everyone else is away? Start a driveway sealing company that seals cracks to extend the longevity of the driveway.

Purchase your basic materials and expand once you have more capital to reinvest.

IDEA NO. 268

Charge Electric Scooters

You can make extra cash by charging electric scooters. The scooter-sharing companies rely on "an army of independent contractors" to locate scooters that need juice, charge them overnight and release them the next morning.

Over time, you can get more supplies if you establish yourself as a consistent and reliable charger.

IDEA NO. 269

Create Content Around Your Job

Start creating content around your everyday job. Whether you work at a sandwich shop or a pizzeria, your day to day life may be fascinating to the internet.

There are so many unique examples of fast-food workers who have gone viral on social media. Why not give it a shot?

IDEA NO. 270

Audio Networking

There are tons of social platforms and websites to directly network with entrepreneurs and creatives in real-time.

Grow a following on platforms of this nature, which will lead you to tons of opportunities in the future.

IDEA NO. 271

Cake Pops

Who doesn't love a delicious cake pop? Start a cake pop business and offer them as custom party favors. Make unique and customized designs and showcase your skills to your customers through online platforms.

Cake pops are a desirable dessert and fun to make!

IDEA NO. 272

Car Magnets

Start a car magnet business that creates custom magnets for businesses, special events and fundraisers. You can help other companies to advertise and grow their business on the go.

Consider pairing this with some extra services to keep you busy year-roundlives

IDEA NO. 273

Candy Business

Are you a candy fanatic? Purchase candy in bulk and sell it for a profit! You can even make customized designs and sell them for higher prices.

Consider selling up a stand at a populated area such as a football stadium, baseball field or even near the grocery store.

IDEA NO. 274

Eyelash Business

Are you into beauty products? There is tons of information online on how to go about starting an eyelash business.

Create fun videos following trends online to show off your latest products. Use social media to extend your businesses reach.

IDEA NO. 275

Shape Surfboards

Are you into surfing? If so, start shaping your own boards and selling them for profit.

Leverage social media to advertise your products. Start making surfing content and slowly start promoting your boards through your channels.

IDEA NO. 276

Birthday Chalkboard

Start a business where you deliver birthday messages on a chalkboard. Use your artistic skills to create colorful designs that will attract the younger audience.

Once you have a website where customers can fill out a form and the designs they want, use the power of Tik Tok to leverage your business.

IDEA NO. 277

Cosmetic Business

Start a cosmetic brand that fashionably sells makeup and nail polish.

People always love looking good so leverage your website to run ads on a targeted audience to convert to sales.

IDEA NO. 278

Snow Cone Business

A Snow Cone business is an IDEA NO.1 candidate for your summer side-hustle. The margins are incredible, you get to be outside soaking up the sun, and you're giving people a constant stream of sugary ice.

Set up shop near local sports games or on a busy street to offer your service.

IDEA NO. 279

Funkie Ties

Instead of people wearing a plain black tie, start a business where you create funky designs that brighten up someone's day with funny quotes.

Create a website and start funneling traffic through social media by creating content and showing off the ties.

IDEA NO. 280

Spray Paint Picture

Use your artistic skills to create your own spray paint art.

Start listing your products on Etsy and post videos on social media to build your brand awareness so eventually you can sell your own artwork on your website.

IDEA NO. 281

Snow Globes

Create a business where you start making homemade snow globes. Make unique items, as with most collectibles; the rarer the item and the better its condition, the more money you're likely to make.

Be unique and have different designs or quotes in your snow globe to stand out and have the best results.

IDEA NO. 282

Mini Hand Held Mirrors

Create a business around cute mini mirrors for your customers to place in their rooms.

Decorate the mini mirrors by adding sparkles and gems around the borders and show off your final products on social media.

IDEA NO. 283

Special Jeans

Use your artistic creativity to create a brand where you customize jeans. Make unique and customized designs, either using colors or other materials.

You can start sewing new patches of clothes, adding gems or even painting them to make your jeans stand out.

IDEA NO. 284

Skateboards

If you like skating, create a brand where you build homemade skateboards and sell them for profit. You can make unique designs depending on your audience and region.

Use the power of social media to market your products to the right niche.

IDEA NO. 285

Slime Business

No one can deny that slime is satisfying to play with. Making it is easy, and there is always a market for cute and colorful slimes online.

To compete with your competition, make sure to be unique and offer over the top slimes that no one else is offering.

IDEA NO. 286

Custom Clock Business

Start a business that allows you to put logos, photos or designs on the face of a clock.

If your business starts to take off, consider expanding to watch faces too.

IDEA NO. 287

Organic Deodorant

Let's face it, we all need deodorant, so we don't reek of body odor. Consider starting a deodorant brand made from organic ingredients that is healthier than typical brands.

The natural products industry is booming, and your business could be the next big one!

IDEA NO. 288

Regrouting Services

Into odd jobs and handyman work? Lots of people need their tile and tubs regrouted after a few years. Create a business that cleans and regrouts tile, so it looks brand new.

Start small and expand as you get more clients.

IDEA NO. 289

Fidget Devices

Start a business that sells trendy fidget devices. Find trendy fidgets and sell them to those looking for an antidote for attention deficit hyperactivity disorder, anxiety and autism.

Fidget spinners and other fidget devices are a hot market. Leverage social media to create viral videos with your products.

IDEA NO. 290

Modded Bikes

Love building things? Learn how to garner energy with either electricity or gasoline.

Once you have a battery/motor, figure out a design for combining the two. You'd be surprised as to how little power you need to spin a wheel.

IDEA NO. 291

Flower Delivery,

Partner with local florists and offers to deliver their flowers to customers for a small fee.

With big events and birthdays, you are bound to get some good tips!

IDEA NO. 292

Beach Set-up Rental

Live near a beach? Offer an easier way to go to the beach where vacationers can play a small fee to have a full beach set-up stocked with drinks and snacks ready on the beach for a fee.

Dragging coolers, umbrellas and chairs is a hassle especially when it's hot out!

IDEA NO. 293

Real Estate Signs

Partner with a local real estate office and have them outsource all their signage placements to you. You can deliver them to the consumer's residence and install them in the yard or up over the garage or doorway.

There are constantly new signs and old signs going out, so you are bound to be busy.

IDEA NO. 294

Mailbox Install

Everyone needs a mailbox. Start a business that installs new mailboxes and replaces old ones too.

Charge a fee for the mailbox and an additional fee for the service of installing it and removing the previous one.

IDEA NO. 295

Subscription-Based newsletter

Pick any unique topic you have an interest in. Start writing a weekly piece on that topic.

Find/Gain a community through social media marketing/advertisements, where you can charge a monthly fee. (ex. $1 a month)

IDEA NO. 296

Sell Digital Artwork

Digital products are the easiest way to make money with digital art online. You can start selling digital art online to earn a passive income, outside of print on demand services and direct marketing, which does not usually apply to art-based products.

You can mint your art using OceanSea and list your Minted NFT on a Marketplace for Buyers. (Mintable, OceanSea, etc.)

IDEA NO. 297

Sell Tropical Fish

Learn to breed/take care of specific fish in an Aquarium. Some fish are more expensive/more in-demand than others. Have your fish breed.

You could sell the offspring to a local pet store. Or set up a website/marketplace to attract specific customers. You'd now be responsible for the shipping/packaging.

IDEA NO. 298

Clam Business

Love spending the summer at the beach? Plant clam seedlings in the bay on your property/legal area.

Once these clams age, you can harvest them. Afterwards, connect and strike a deal with local vendors/restaurants.

IDEA NO. 299

Start a Band

Are you musically talented? Look for other hard-working musicians you'd get along with.

After creating music together, promote and book your own shows. Start locally and then grow your audience/connections. Social media can be a huge help with this.

IDEA NO. 300

Backpack Business

Design unique, affordable backpacks. Do your research and include current or vintage Pop-Culture art.

Set up a website where customers can find a price and visual of the product. Market to the High School and younger demographic.

IDEA NO. 301

Start a Copywriting Business

Good at writing? Many companies will pay handsomely for someone to do the writing part of their advertising/marketing.

After providing your writing expertise, start taking on more clients. Have previous jobs recommend you to future clients and expand at your own pace.

IDEA NO. 302

Language Tutor

Love to teach and are fluent in 1 or more languages? There's never been a larger interest in foreign cultures.

More and more people are traveling and learning about foreign cultures. Multiple companies offer part-time work for teaching online classes.

IDEA NO. 303

Sell Christmas Trees

Find a Christmas tree wholesaler/farm. Also, find a local out of season sports field/plot of land. Speak to the town about renting if it's not private property.

Buy the trees in bulk from the wholesaler. Mark up the prices and store/sell the trees from that property.

IDEA NO. 304

Martial Arts Studio

Have an advanced background in MMA and love teaching? Start your own online MMA classes. Advertise/Market using social media.

Eventually, save enough capital and invest in a small property; to use as a physical studio. Preferably in an up and coming/established community. Target and grow the MMA community in that area.

IDEA NO. 305

Lacrosse Trainer

Have you played, or are you knowledgeable in lacrosse? Lacrosse is currently one of the newest/hottest sports in the United States.

More and more parents are willing to pay for their children to learn this sport now. The top-ranked college teams are all prestigious universities. Therefore, parents might see this as an investment for a possible scholarship.

IDEA NO. 306

Lining Sports Fields

Does your town have sports fields? Chances are, they need to be lined up during the season. Usually, different parents on the team have to do this.

Communicate with the local sports teams and work out a deal to maintain and paint the fields.

IDEA NO. 307

Open Source Restaurant Review Database

Start listing your town's local restaurants. Allow customers to make write-ups on their experience.

The market is a more community niche database. Specific to your town and surrounding areas.

IDEA NO. 308

Sell Pumpkins

Love quick cash and Halloween? Buy a bunch of pumpkins from a wholesale/farm. You can sell pumpkins according to their weight and size.

Put out fliers and posts in your town's Facebook group. Offer cheap quality pumpkins.

IDEA NO. 309

Reaction Channel

Are you always the one cracking jokes in front of your friends? Start a comedic reactionary page. Have your viewers invested/drawn to your reaction to another video?

It doesn't always need to be comedic. Find whatever niche/style your personality does well with.

IDEA NO. 310

Czy Blankets

Know how to sew? Love designing art? Combine them by making handmade blankets.

Add a unique design to each and every blanket. List/promote these on social media.

IDEA NO. 311

Collectible Business

People love collecting unique items. Pick a few different collectibles you are passionate about and buy and resell them for a profit.

Whether this is figurines, antiques or coins, lots of collectibles have some serious resale value!

IDEA NO. 312

Custom Wood Pens

Are you skilled at woodworking? Start a pen company that creates handmade pens of immense quality. You need to decide the rates depending upon the effort and time consumed.

Sell these locally and on websites such as Etsy, where you can connect with an audience looking for handmade items.

IDEA NO. 313

News Company

Love current events? Start an independent news company by reporting on events and stories that you genuinely find interest in.

Although the news industry is flooded with massive corporations, if you put a cool spin on your reporting, you may just be the next big thing.

IDEA NO. 314

Research Business

Excellent at researching specific topics? Start a business where companies hire you to research products, niches or topics for a set cost.

Whether this is gathering information, data or in-depth research, this could be a profitable hustle.

IDEA NO. 315

Healthy Grass Company

Start a company that waters your grass with a certain formula to ensure healthy growth and minimize weeds.

If you live in a prosperous town, a grass watering company could be extremely lucrative.

IDEA NO. 316

College Decor Business

Interested in interior design and room decor? Start a business catered towards college students that sells cute and trendy decor.

Promote your business on social media platforms and give influencer marketing a shot!

IDEA NO. 317

Handmade Earrings

Are you a jewelry fanatic? Start a business that creates, markets and sells handmade earrings online!

Use social media and handmade websites such as Etsy when marketing your products to your target audience.

IDEA NO. 318

White Noise Website

Does white noise help you sleep at night? Start a website that provides free white noise and monetize by positioning advertisements on the site.

This is a great business model as people stay on the site for hours and continually come back daily.

IDEA NO. 319

Framed Art

Intrigued by art? Start a framed art business that sells digital or physical art pieces in unique frames.

Offer worldwide shipping and market your products with some cool photos and watch the sales come in.

IDEA NO. 320

Custom Mugs

Who doesn't love a hot cup of coffee in the morning? Better yet- in a custom mug with a photo or logo on it! Start a custom mug business by reaching out to businesses to see if they are looking for promotional items.

Promotional items are a huge market especially if you can make them with a fast turnaround!

IDEA NO. 321

Artist Murals

If you can create large murals with spray paint or other art supplies, a mural business might be for you!

Murals are always in demand in cities and densely populated areas!

IDEA NO. 322

Photoshop Family Photos

This may seem silly, but if you are a photoshop expert, starting a business where you can edit family photos to remove unwanted people or background distractions can be lucrative.

Market your business showing how you have helped other clients through leveraging before and after photos. Market your services globally on freelance sites such as Fiverr, Upwork and others.

IDEA NO. 323

Shoe Cleaning Business

Are you a sneakerhead? Start a shoe cleaning business by helping some of your friends restore their shoes to a better condition.

Once your business takes off, consider expanding by offering your own sneaker cleaning solution and brushes.

IDEA NO. 324

Paint Shoes

Another option for sneakerheads is customizing shoes with paint and stencils. Watch lots of YouTube videos and practice on old shoes before you market your services.

Leverage digital platforms and tradeshows as a means of getting the word out about your services.

IDEA NO. 325

Build PC's

Are you an expert at building complex gaming PC's? Why not start a business helping others build custom setups to best fit their needs and wants.

Have them purchase all the supplies and charge a service fee based on the amount of time you estimate this project will take you.

IDEA NO. 326

Singer

Have a great voice? Monetize this talent with recording and posting yourself online. Many different places offer different "pay per view" rates for your content.

Keep posting your covers/songs to grow and market your own brand on social media.

IDEA NO. 327

House Mats

Most households have/would be interested in a doormat. What better way to greet your visitors than a unique doormat.

Incorporate comedic, loving, informational, relatable messages on each doormat.

IDEA NO. 328

Custom Controllers

With the gaming industry growing each and every day, try and dip your toes in. Design customizable controllers that people in your town/grade would like.

Build a customer base through social media, Xbox Live, PlayStation network, word of mouth.

IDEA NO. 329

Christmas Light Service

Are you a hard worker? Love the Christmas season? Offer a Christmas light service to your neighbors/town. Your Christmas business can make money by charging customers to install, service and takedown decorative lights during the holiday season.

Offer your customer a better aesthetic and a cheap price. Be more than just the usual pay per service.

IDEA NO. 330

Hot Chocolate Stand

Have a busy downtown? Set Up a hot chocolate stand in a high traffic area during the cold months. Open your own stand where people come when they are cold to get a delicious warm cup of hot chocolate.

Sell your Hot Chocolate at a lower price than your town's Starbucks.

IDEA NO. 331

Puppet Service

Have a unique voice? Learn how to perform voice-over skits with puppets. You will require little costs for start-up and higher customer retention rates.

This can also be a viable option for a creative personality who doesn't feel comfortable in front of the camera.

IDEA NO. 332

Cruise Booker

Set Up an online website/social media page that connects followers to cruises. You can compare cruise rates for your customers and provide a feasible package to them.

With everything opening back up, travel has become a growing industry.

IDEA NO. 333

Locksmith Services

There is still a need to lock up physical items. You can be one of the few locksmiths in your area. You can make keys, install locks, and even crack the occasional safe after getting some experience.

A needed industry that's looking for help is always a good choice to choose for an industry.

IDEA NO. 334

Freelance Researcher

There's plenty of companies that need research for their websites. Companies have to keep innovating and learning about their industry every day.

Some companies will even pay for you to research and provide feedback for certain tasks/jobs.

IDEA NO. 335

Content Marketing Strategist

Have a background in the content making? Use your expertise to grow other accounts. You can publicize a business using content to drive up sales of products, services or generate leads.

People will pay a premium for Social media expertise. This is a huge industry, and you can earn a hefty amount if you know it properly.

IDEA NO. 336

Public Relations Consultant

Have a very good work ethic? Love the entertainment industry? Work as a Stars #2. You can become a freelancer and work for different companies as a part-timer.

Take care of their publicity and anything media related with their client.

IDEA NO. 337

Diaper Delivery

Narrow down on unique delivery service. Sell a convenient service to the young family. Many times their schedule is all over the place. Never have to go to the store after running out of diapers.

Perform some research before you start a diaper delivery service. Find out who your competition is, what they charge for their service, what they do well, and what you think you can do better. It might be that there is a lot of competition in your area, or you may find that you will be the only game in town!

IDEA NO. 338

Travel Concierge Service

Offer a more person to person experience for someone looking to travel and make their journey more adventurous. You can earn a hefty income as traveling and tourism are becoming more popular, affordable, and easier.

Make an easy to use service that connects users to hotels, airlines, etc.

IDEA NO. 339

Graffiti Removal

Love restoring things? Help out your community by cleaning up other peoples graffiti.

Many businesses/towns deal with graffiti ruining their property. You can offer to repaint their area and charge extra for this additional service.

IDEA NO. 340

YouTube Marketing Strategist

Learn/study the youtube algorithm. Bring on clients and test your hypothesis.

Hopefully, the results pay off, and your clients' accounts grow.

IDEA NO. 341

Local Business Promoter

Start a local blog to help promote local businesses such as restaurants, coffee shops and other service-based businesses.

In the beginning, most businesses will give you free items in return for promotion but once you build a strong enough following, you will be able to monetize in other ways.

IDEA NO. 342

Barber App

Create an app that connects barbers with those looking for a haircut. On the app, you can pick from 1000's hairstyles and see reviews for local barbershops.

When customers book directly through your app, you can charge the barbershop a service fee to make money.

IDEA NO. 343

Custom Socks

Start a fun custom sock business using sublimation printing. Find a reliable supplier of materials and create your own designs to sell on your website.

In addition to having your own designs, allow customers to make their own socks with photos, logos and colors of their choice.

IDEA NO. 344

Men's Accessories

Men's fashion accessories are becoming more and more popular. Start a trendy men's accessory brand that includes rings, necklaces, bracelets and other fun ways to become more stylish.

This can be a great niche business. Focus on online selling and marketing your business in unique ways on social media.

IDEA NO. 345

Extreme Couponing Site

Are you obsessed with getting free items or deals at your favorite stores? Start a website that shares the latest and greatest deals with your audience.

Monetize your website through advertisements, affiliate links and premium members.

IDEA NO. 346

Town Wear

Start an online store that sells merchandise with your town's name on it. People always love wearing custom clothing.

Be careful not to use any logos or slogans that could get you in trouble for infringing on a trademark.

IDEA NO. 347

Edging

If you are into the landscaping scene, edging is a popular service where you essentially dig out the flower beds in one's yard and make a more prominent divot between the grass and the dirt.

Offering edging as a service alone or include it when you do a mulching job!

IDEA NO. 348

Key Cutting Machine

Purchase a key cutting machine and reach out to local businesses to see if you can place it in or outside their store. Split the profits, and it's a win-win for everyone.

Making duplicates of a key promptly is always something consumers will need!

IDEA NO. 349

Affiliate Travel Site

Start an affiliate travel site and drive as much traffic as possible through various social media platforms. You will earn a commission every time someone books a trip through your site.

Affiliate sites can be extremely profitable if you promote them correctly!

IDEA NO. 350

Custom Care Packages

Are you good at making aesthetically pleasing care packages? Start a care package company that curates unique gifts for special occasions such as birthdays, anniversaries and more.

This can be a lucrative business, especially if you market yourself well; word of mouth will spread rapidly!

IDEA NO. 351

Bread Delivery Subscription

Partner with some local bakeries and start a website where locals can subscribe to get a fresh loaf of bread delivered to their house once a week.

Split the profits with the bakery. Word will spread fast.

IDEA NO. 352

Vlogger

Is your life fast-paced and extremely interesting? Start vlogging weekly to capture some of the craziest moments of your week.

Post your chopped up videos on YouTube to see if you can attract a following.

IDEA NO. 353

Education Website

Start a subscription-based website that allows you to receive unlimited access to educational materials on a certain subject when you are a member.

Subscription business models are the future! Consider starting one

IDEA NO. 354

Coloring Books

Leverage self-publishing websites to create coloring books in profitable niches on Amazon. If you aren't an expert artist, you can outsource the artwork on freelance sites for an affordable price.

Coloring books can be a great way to earn passive income if you understand creating and market them properly.

IDEA NO. 355

Crabbing Business

Live near the beach? Learn how to optimize the number of crabs you can catch each day. Find some hidden spots that hold or attract crabs.

Sells these crabs to local restaurants/farmers markets.

IDEA NO. 356

Pong Theme Tables

Know how to build a table? Add some paint and a pop-culture design to it.

Focus on marketing and advertising through social media.

IDEA NO. 357

Name Towels

Use your creativity to create soft, comfortable and yet unique towels. Allow your customers to be able to customize or add any writing to their order. Provide different sizes and colors to attract customers from every age group.

Incorporate recyclable materials. It will make your brand unique and stand you out among the crowd.

IDEA NO. 358

Video Brochure

Offer an interactive online brochure. Customers can be more in touch and feel the destination more than just ink on paper.

This has you stand out compared to traditional physical brochures.

IDEA NO. 359

Office Plant Maintenance

Many people think of maintaining their plants as an inconvenience. Go office to office asking them if they'd hire a service to maintain their plants.

Plants offer a great vibe to any room.

IDEA NO. 360

Valet Parking

Ask every local restaurant if they would be interested in a valet service. Find a nearby area to park the cars.

Make sure you have built a good reputation before expanding your business. People take their cars and any damage to them very seriously.

IDEA NO. 361

Pet-Food and Supplies Home Delivery

Narrow down your customer base to this specific niche. Market your service on social media using hashtags that include pets.

Offer a cheaper alternative for these customers instead of them using a Walmart, doordash etc.

IDEA NO. 362

Greeting Cards

If you can write and/or have design skills, you can start making money online by creating and selling greeting cards. If you have the writing skills to create sentimental and appealing verses, quotes, poems or paragraphs suitable for greeting cards. In that case, you definitely fit the bill and can start making money online from your skills.

You can approach online marketplaces to sell your product.

IDEA NO. 363

Travel Writer

Enjoy traveling and love to write? Many companies would love others to review their products. Monetize your reviews and keep traveling to write more reviews.

You can even become a freelancer and start a travel blog. You can start pitching tourism boards, brands you like, or tour companies with no content on their website.

IDEA NO. 364

Running Coach

Are you an advanced runner? Love helping others? Start giving tips and train people.

After a few successful clients, expand your list. You can advertise your brand by starting a blog or even work for a running store.

IDEA NO. 365

Voice Acting

Have a creative mind? Hate being in front of cameras? Voice acting may be for you.

This is perfect for somebody trying to get into the industry, especially those who aren't used to the cameras.